SMART STRUCTURES

DAMS

Julie Richards

A+

This edition first published in 2004 in the United States of America by Smart Apple Media.

Smart Apple Media
1980 Lookout Drive
North Mankato
Minnesota 56003

Library of Congress Cataloging-in-Publication Data
Richards, Julie.
    Dams / by Julie Richards.
    p. cm. — (Smart structures)
    Includes index.
    Contents: Dams as structures—Looking closely at dams—The parts of a dam—Building materials—Dam design—Building a dam—Working dams—Dams that went wrong—Amazing dams—Using models to learn about structures.
    ISBN 1-58340-345-0
    1. Dams—Juvenile literature. [1. Dams.] I. Title.
    TC540.R53 2003
    627'.8—dc21   2002044631

First Edition
9 8 7 6 5 4 3 2 1

First published in 2003 by
MACMILLAN EDUCATION AUSTRALIA PTY LTD
627 Chapel Street, South Yarra, Australia 3141

Associated companies and representatives throughout the world.

Edited by Anna Fern
Text design by Cristina Neri, Canary Graphic Design
Cover design by Cristina Neri, Canary Graphic Design
Layout by Nina Sanadze
Illustrations by Margaret Hastie, IKON Computergraphics
Photo research by Legend Images

Printed in Thailand

Acknowledgements
The author and the publisher are grateful to the following for permission to reproduce copyright material:

Cover photograph: Kariba Dam, courtesy of Reuters.

Ancient Art & Architecture, p. 10; Australian Picture Library/Corbis, pp. 13, 14, 21, 23 (top); Corbis Digital Stock, pp. 5 (bottom right), 20; Getty Images, pp. 4, 5 (top right), 8, 19, 22, 24, 28; The Kobal Collection, p. 17; Brian Parker, p. 5 (bottom left); Photolibrary.com, p. 23 (bottom); Reuters, pp. 5 (top left), 9, 11, 16, 18, 25, 26, 27; Southern California LEGO Train Club, design by Paul Thomas, Riverside, California, photo by Thomas Michon, Irvine, California, p. 30.

CONTENTS

KEY WORDS

When a word is printed in **bold** you can look up its meaning in the key words box on the same page. You can also look up the meaning of words in the glossary on page 31.

DAMS AS STRUCTURES

A **structure** is made up of many different parts joined together. The shapes of the parts and the way they are joined together help a structure to stand up and do the job for which it has been designed. The **materials** used to make a structure can be made stronger or weaker, depending on their shape and how they are put together.

Dams are made by humans, but some animals, such as the **beaver**, also build dams. Water is vital to our survival. Even though three-quarters of Earth is covered by water, some parts of the world are still very dry. Sometimes there is too little water, while at other times there is too much. For as long as people have wanted to control water, they have built dams. Dams are useful for:

- collecting and storing water
- creating a source of clean, safe drinking water
- **irrigating** crops
- controlling rivers, lakes, and seas to prevent flooding
- making a river **channel** deeper so that ships can travel safely
- making a type of electricity called hydro-electricity.

This beaver dam was built by ramming sticks into the mud of the river-bed and then placing small trees and branches across them. Small boulders are placed on the structure to stop it from collapsing. Mud is used like glue to keep all the parts stuck together, making the dam watertight. Humans have copied many of the features of a beaver dam.

Types of dams

Dams come in different shapes and sizes. There are four types of dams made by humans:

- arch dams
- **gravity** dams
- **embankment** dams
- **buttress** dams.

The type of dam that is built depends on why it is needed and the place where it is to be built.

The Kariba arch dam generates hydro-electricity and controls flooding on the border of Zimbabwe and Zambia, in Africa.

The Grand Coulee Dam, in the United States, is a gravity dam.

The Aswan High Dam, in Egypt, is an embankment dam. Can you see how its shape is different from the arch dam?

The Dalles Dam, in the U.S., is a buttress dam.

If you look very closely at a dam, you will notice:

- the different parts which have been joined together to build the dam
- the shapes of these parts.

Dams must support extremely heavy loads. Earthquakes can cause a dam to crack. It is important that the different parts are made in the right shapes and joined together in the right way, or the dam will not be safe.

KEY WORDS

engineers people who design and build large structures

stable something that will not wobble or fall

Dam shapes

About 400 years ago, **engineers** began to study what made a structure stay up. They learned that large, heavy structures could only be made strong and **stable** by using certain shapes such as triangles and arches put together in a particular pattern. Some shapes are stronger than others. Rectangles, arches, and triangles are the strongest shapes that are used to build big structures, but they all have their breaking point.

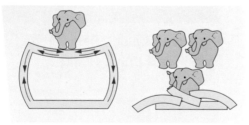

Rectangle

One elephant on a rectangle makes the top side bend. The weight of three elephants causes the top side to break.

Arch

The weight of three elephants on an arch spreads along the curve to the ground below. The weight of six elephants causes the sides to spread apart and collapse.

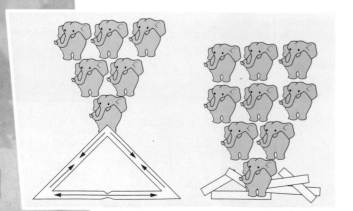

Triangle

The weight of six elephants on a triangle causes the two top sides to squeeze together and the bottom side to pull apart. The triangle is the strongest shape, but a herd of elephants makes the bottom side stretch so much that it snaps in half.

Arches

The arch is a very strong shape. Inside your foot there is a bone that forms an arch. It supports most of the weight of your body when you are standing. Dams need to be extremely strong because water cannot stay in one place by itself. Water always spreads out and flows downhill unless it is held in place by a solid barrier. The water behind a dam wall is constantly pushing against it. Most dam walls are built in the shape of an arch because it is a very strong shape.

Can weaker shapes be made stronger?

Rectangles are not as strong as triangles. Rectangles can be made stronger by using extra pieces of building material to make them into triangles. An extra piece like this is called a **brace**. Triangles are the strongest, stiffest, and most stable of all the shapes.

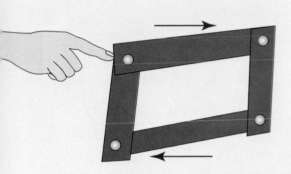

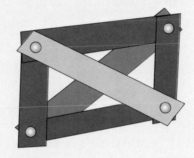

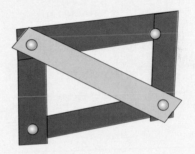

The sides of a rectangle are weak and can be easily moved about.

Fixing two pieces of material to a rectangle makes it stiffer and stronger.

One of the extra pieces can be taken away without weakening the rectangle.

Invisible shapes

The shapes used in a dam cannot always be seen because they are hidden inside the dam structure or beneath the surface of the water. But triangles are used to stabilize and strengthen the rectangular wall used in some types of dams.

All dams have a wall, **foundations**, pipes, and spillways. Without these important parts, a dam cannot do the job for which it has been designed.

Wall

The main part of every dam is the dam wall itself, which holds back the water in the **reservoir**. The wall is usually quite a simple structure made from **concrete** strengthened with steel bars, soil, or rock. Some dams are a combination of more than one dam type. For example, part of the dam wall may be an arch with an embankment dam wall at either end.

Foundations

The foundations of a dam are like the roots of a tree that go deep into the ground. The weight of a large amount of water in a dam is extremely heavy and its weight keeps trying to push it further down into the ground. The weight of the water behind the dam wall is immense and this also pushes against the dam wall. The foundations are usually made of **bedrock**. The foundations support the enormous weight of the dam by spreading it through the ground. If you have ever tried to walk on fresh snow, you will know how easy it is to sink and fall over. If you wear snowshoes or skis, they spread your weight out evenly across the snow so that you can stand up. Foundations work in the same way.

KEY WORDS

foundations a firm base upon which a structure is built

reservoir a lake for storing water until it is needed

concrete a building material made by mixing cement and sand or gravel with water

bedrock solid rock beneath the soil

The dam wall is supported on deep bedrock foundations. This dam gets added strength from its arches.

Stopping leaks

All dams leak a little. Even hard, solid rocks have tiny cracks or holes in them that let water seep through. Sometimes, water gets in between the tiny particles that make up the rock. All dams have a waterproof barrier beneath them called a cut-off, which is usually made with a mixture of water and **cement**, called grout.

Spillways, pipes, and channels

Spillways, pipes, and channels control the flow of water through the dam. All dams have a spillway, which lets water out of the reservoir if the water level rises too high. Without a spillway, the water would eventually flow over the top of the dam. If water ran continually down the dam wall, the water would wear away the base of the dam, perhaps causing it to collapse. The spillway is either a channel at the side of the dam, a channel in the **face** of the dam, or tunnels blasted through the rock next to the dam.

The spillway on the Itaipu Dam, between Brazil and Paraguay in South America, empties several swimming pools of water every second. The water can travel up to 62 miles (100 km) per hour.

Water supply

Every dam has a system of pipes which allow water to flow from the reservoir straight into the river below the dam, into the water supply, irrigation channels, or a hydro-electric power station.

KEY WORDS

cement an ingredient in concrete which makes the concrete harden like stone

face the front of the dam

BUILDING MATERIALS

The first dam builders used the natural materials they found around them. An early dam was usually made from earth, clay, and rock. When engineers began to study what made a structure stay up, they developed new materials which allowed them to build bigger, stronger dams that could hold enough water for a large population. Today, most dams are made of concrete and steel. Embankment dams are still built from natural materials such as gravel, sand, clay, and chunks of solid rock.

Concrete

Concrete is the most important material for building modern dams. Concrete is a mixture of cement, water, sand, and gravel. The wet, runny mixture is poured into molds so that it can be shaped before it dries to become hard and extremely strong. A piece of concrete four inches (10 cm) square could support a 33-ton (30-t) weight. Concrete, however, cracks quite easily when it is stretched.

The Grand Coulee Dam, in central Washington, contains 22 million tons (20 million t) of concrete!

◀ **People living in Yemen built this ancient dam in the 700s.**

Steel

Steel is made mostly of iron and is used in many large structures. Steel is strong, lighter than iron, and **flexible**. A steel cable as thick as your finger could lift a 33-ton (30-t) truck!

Although concrete is strong enough to resist squashing, it cannot stretch without cracking. Bunches of steel bars can be added to concrete and used in the parts of the dam that need to stretch. This material is called **reinforced** concrete. Reinforced concrete is used in the foundations and beams of many large structures.

▲ Reinforced concrete is being used to make strong water pipes for this dam.

Waterproofing materials

Engineers add special kinds of cement to their concrete to make it waterproof or resistant to the **corrosive** chemicals that can be found in some river water. Cement and water are also used to make grout. Grout is used to make earth or loose rock beneath a dam waterproof. Embankment dams use clay as a waterproofing material because it is made up of tiny particles which are very, very close together. Water cannot trickle between these particles like it can through the larger, loose particles of soil, or the holes in soft rocks.

This cross-section of an embankment dam shows how it is waterproofed.

Roadway

Embankment

Rocks protect against waves

Waterproof core

DAM DESIGN

Engineers must do a lot of research to make sure that the right type of dam is designed. The type of dam that is chosen will depend on what it is to be used for, how big a population it is to serve, and whether or not the ground is suitable. There are four types of human-made dams:

- gravity
- arch
- buttress
- embankment.

Gravity dams

A gravity dam is an enormously heavy wall of concrete. The wall is so heavy that the water cannot push the dam forward or topple it over. The bottom of the Hoover Dam wall, between Nevada and Arizona, is as thick as two playing fields measured end to end.

Arch dams

An arch dam has a thin concrete wall which curves out into the reservoir. The weight of the water pushing against the wall spreads out around the dam and into the ground at the sides. The Hoover Dam is a gravity dam, but it also has an arch-shaped wall. The Hoover Dam wall is strong enough not to need the arch shape, but the designers thought that people might feel safer if the dam was built that way.

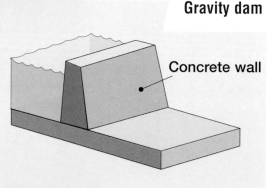

Gravity dam

Concrete wall

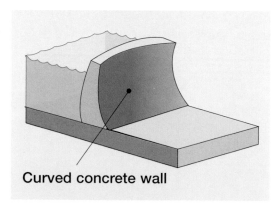

Curved concrete wall

Arch dam. The concrete wall curves in more than one way. This gives the dam added strength.

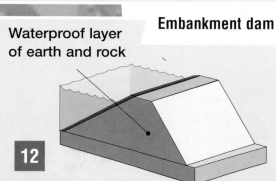

Waterproof layer of earth and rock

Embankment dam

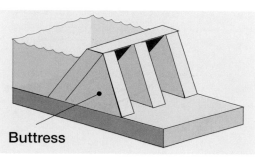

Buttress

Buttress dam. You can see the triangles that form the buttresses supporting the dam wall.

Buttress dams

The wall of a buttress dam has a sloping face. The water pushes against the wall and presses the dam wall into the ground. Heavy triangular walls, called buttresses, support the wall from behind to stop the water from toppling the dam over. The Daniel Johnson Dam, in Canada, has 14 buttresses linked by arches, with two huge buttresses in the middle.

Embankment dams

An embankment dam is an immense earth or rock bank, with gently sloping faces. It works very much like a combined gravity and buttress dam because it is very heavy, and relies on the strength of the triangular shape of its wall to act like a buttress.

An embankment dam needs to be a lot thicker than other types of dams. Enough rock to build 17 Great Pyramids was used to build the Aswan High Dam in Egypt.

Earth and rock are not watertight like concrete, so an embankment dam needs a layer of waterproof material on its face or inside, to stop water from trickling through.

Dams can be made up of different types of dams joined end to end. This one has an embankment dam in the center and a buttress dam at each end.

Where to build?

Geologists look at samples of soil to find out:

- if the rock layers beneath the dam site are strong enough to support the foundations
- whether or not the rock is waterproof
- if there is any earthquake activity.

Earthquakes can crack a dam, making it leak or, even worse, collapse and cause terrible flooding. A dam can also cause an earthquake because the weight of the water it contains presses down hard on the rock layers underneath. If it presses too hard, the rock layers can move, triggering an earthquake.

▲ **Engineers make a model of the dam and the reservoir to help them explain the dam structure.**

Different dams for different needs

Embankment dams are usually built in wide valleys where the bedrock is buried under layers of soft ground such as clay or **silt**.

Concrete dams are normally built in narrow valleys where the bedrock is close to the surface. To build a concrete dam across a wide valley would be too expensive because the bedrock would be much deeper and the dam a lot wider.

A dam which will be used to irrigate crops or to provide drinking water needs to be built where it will form a large reservoir.

A dam which will be used to generate hydro-electricity has to be built high up, where the rush of falling water is strongest.

Bypassing the dam

A dam is a barrier designed to block a river. Where the river is important to the environment, or is a waterway that carries ships, the designers must find ways of bypassing the dam.

Canals and locks

A canal is a human-made waterway which can be built alongside the river. Ships can travel through the canal and go around the dam and then back into the river. The water level in the river below the dam is lower than the water level behind the dam, so the ship is lowered inside a lock.

The ship is moving through a lock so that it can bypass a weir. ▶

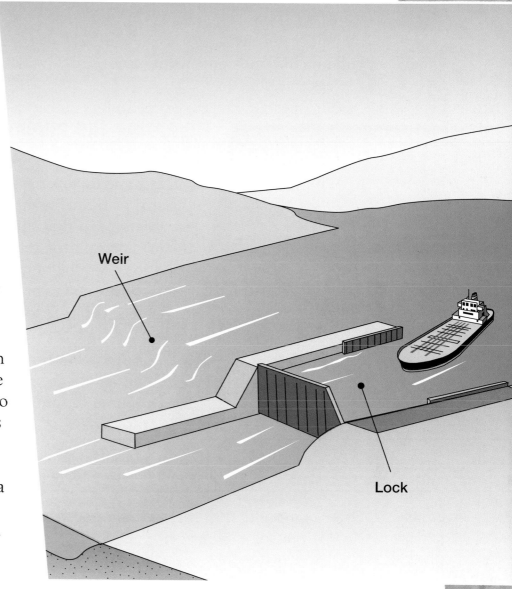

A lock is a short section of canal with a set of gates at each end. Once the ship is inside the lock, the gates can be opened to let water out. Doing this lowers the water level inside the lock. The gates are opened and the ship moves out. Locks are like a step in a staircase. By letting water in or out, ships can travel uphill and downhill.

Looking after the environment

Building a dam means blasting and removing enormous amounts of soil and rock and changing the direction of the river. This can damage the environment, driving away wildlife. If their homes and food supply are destroyed, they can never return. The builders repair the environment as much as possible by replacing some of the rock and soil and replanting the area with the trees and grasses that were found there before. Some dams have a fish ladder. A fish ladder is a series of pools built around the dam which are linked by sloping pipes. Fish can travel around the new dam by swimming from pool to pool.

BUILDING A DAM

Building a dam is an enormous job. It can take hundreds of workers many years to finish.

KEY WORDS

temporary for a short time only
groundworks the preparation of the ground for a dam's foundations

Diverting the river

The dam site has to be dry before any work can begin. This is done by diverting the river around the dam. A channel or tunnel is dug around the side of the dam site for the river to flow into. A machine like a crane with a giant scoop on the end of its arm scrapes out the river-bed to make the new channel. When the Hoover Dam was built, the Colorado River was diverted through tunnels as big as four-lane highways that were blasted through solid rock.

A low, **temporary** dam, called a cofferdam, is built across the river, which guides the water to the channel or tunnel. Once the ground has dried out, the digging or **groundworks** can begin.

This river is being diverted to build a hydro-electric dam.

Groundworks

There is still a lot of digging to be done before the dam building can start. Monster earth-moving machines called power shovels use their room-sized buckets to dig deep into the earth. The teeth on the digging and scraping machines are designed to sharpen themselves as they dig into the ground until they need replacing. The loose earth is loaded into dump trucks as high as houses and taken away. Where solid rock needs to be removed, it is first broken up with explosives. The explosives are stuffed into holes drilled into the rock and are exploded by remote control.

Water pressure

All·dams are wider at the bottom than they are at the top. This is because the water at the bottom of a reservoir is squashed down by the water above it. The water at the bottom is under a lot more pressure and pushes against the dam wall. The deeper the water, the stronger the dam has to be. If there are any cracks in the wall, the water will force its way into them, making them bigger and weakening the structure. A dam that is not strong enough or properly waterproofed can spring a leak.

This still photograph from the film *Superman* shows a dam bursting. This is not real, but it does give you an idea of the immense power of moving water.

Waterproofing

Waterproofing is done before the dam wall is begun. Trenches are dug and filled with waterproofing material such as concrete or clay to stop underground water from seeping into the dam. Rocks that allow water to seep through are drilled and grout is pumped into the holes. The grout spreads through the ground and sets very hard. Waterproofing is especially important for embankment dams because they are made of earth and rock instead of concrete.

Building a concrete dam

All dams, except embankment dams, are made of concrete. Large concrete dams contain gigantic amounts of concrete. Delivering the 33 million tons (30 million t) of concrete needed for the Itaipu Dam, on the Brazil–Paraguay border, would have taken two concrete mixers a whole year working every minute of every day. So, a concrete-mixing factory is normally built at the dam site. The concrete is poured into buckets and travels along overhead cables to where it is needed. Wet concrete must be poured into a mold to give it the right shape. The mold is made with wooden sheets or steel plates, called formwork, supported by scaffolding. The reinforcing steel is put in place so that it will be covered when the concrete sets.

Look at the steel reinforcing bars and the heavy equipment needed to build the dam wall.

A concrete dam is built up in layered towers. Each layer is allowed to set before the next one is added. The towers are connected by special joints called keys. Grout is sprayed into the gaps to waterproof the joints. Concrete is sprayed over the joints to make the dam look like one enormous wall. Plastic sheeting stops the concrete from drying too quickly, which can make it crack. As the dam wall is built, the spillways, pipes, and hydro-electric power station are built, too.

Making the reservoir

Once the dam is completed, the temporary cofferdam is removed and the channels diverting the river are filled with concrete. The river returns to its original route, flowing up against the dam wall and eventually forming a reservoir behind it.

Gravity dams

A gravity dam is built in the same way as a concrete dam, except the wall is much thicker at its base. This thickness gives the dam wall a triangular shape and much greater stability to resist the push of the deeper water.

The Grand Coulee gravity dam, completed in 1942, in the U.S., was one of the first dams to use an immense amount of concrete in its wall—enough concrete to build a highway across North America.

The engineers were faced with a problem they had not dealt with before. When the chemicals in wet concrete mix together, they give off heat as it dries. When the concrete cools, it shrinks and, if the shrinkage is not controlled, cracks form. To stop the concrete from shrinking and cracking as it dried, the engineers pumped cold water through a network of pipes inside the concrete to keep it cool as it hardened. If they had left the concrete to cool naturally, it would have taken 200 years!

The Grand Coulee Dam is a concrete gravity dam. ▼

The Hoover Dam is another concrete gravity dam, built between 1933 and 1935. The dam is built across the Colorado River, in the U.S. As the concrete was poured for the Hoover Dam, some of the workers stood inside the formwork and smoothed the wet concrete with their feet before the next bucketful was tipped in. They were called puddlers. A cable craneway was installed so that heavy equipment such as **turbines** and **generators** could be swung across the canyon and lowered into position.

KEY WORDS

turbines machines that spin like wheels when water flows over them

generators machines that make electricity

19

Arch dams

An arch dam has a much thinner concrete wall than a gravity dam because its strength is in its shape. About 400 years ago, Spanish engineers discovered that a curved dam wall is much stronger than a straight one, so the wall could be made of much thinner material. An arch shape is just as strong lying down as it is standing up.

There are not many arch dams in the world because there are few major rivers that pass through narrow rocky gorges. The Kariba Dam, in Africa, is an arch dam. Its reservoir, Lake Kariba, is 173 miles (280 km) long!

Buttress dams

A buttress dam requires much less concrete than a gravity dam, but it needs a lot of extra formwork and steel reinforcing to strengthen it. The first reinforced concrete buttress dam was built in 1903, in the U.S.

Buttress dams are usually built where the soil is not good enough to support a heavier concrete dam. The buttresses are triangular-shaped wedges which support the straight concrete dam wall from behind. The weight of the water is sent down each buttress into the river-bed rather than relying on the ground at the sides to soak it up. Buttresses can be spaced further apart by building arches in between them.

The Daniel Johnson Dam, in Canada, is a very large arch-buttress dam. It is 4,284 feet (1,306 m) long and, at a height of 703 feet (214 m), it is among the highest dams in the world.

◀ **The wedges of this buttress dam hold the water back.**

Embankment dams

Millions of tons of earth and rock are needed to build an embankment dam. Earth and rock are trucked from a **quarry** to the dam site and tipped onto the embankment. Machines that have rollers instead of front wheels press down each layer. Pressing it down like this squashes all the particles of earth and rock tightly together, making it stronger and waterproof. Massive rocks and concrete blocks are added after several layers. These blocks, which are as big as cars, rest against the face of the dam to protect the earth from being washed away by waves.

The development of monster earth-moving equipment means that a large embankment dam can be built more quickly and easily than in the past.

Embankment dams are always built with a gentle slope, and the base of the wall must be at least four times wider than the top. Embankment dams are the oldest and simplest type of dam. They are also the biggest. The Tarbela embankment dam, in Pakistan, was completed in 1977. It is not the longest or highest, but it contains more earth and rock than any other embankment dam in the world.

Rockfill dams

A rockfill dam is an embankment dam built with rocks instead of earth. A rockfill dam is heavier than an earth dam, so it need not be as wide. A layer of clay or concrete is often added to stop water from leaking through the gaps in the rocks. Sometimes, a timber framework is built, to keep the rocks in place, and topped with a concrete cap.

KEY WORDS

quarry a place where stone is removed by digging or blasting

WORKING DAMS

Dams can be very helpful. Just one dam can do many different jobs, such as:

- supply a reliable source of clean drinking water
- irrigate crops
- generate electricity
- control flooding.

In the last 50 years, there have been many enormous dams built on the major rivers of the world. These are called super dams. A super dam can improve the lives of many people in poorer countries.

Unfortunately, while fixing some problems, a large dam can sometimes cause other problems. **Environmentalists** argue that such large dams destroy the natural flow of the river.

The Aswan High Dam, in Egypt, was very helpful to the people living on one part of the Nile River. In the 1980s, it generated enough electricity every year to power one million televisions for 20 years! The farmers were using water from the reservoir to grow twice as many crops as they had grown before the dam was built, and a thriving fishing industry had grown up on the reservoir.

Below the dam, however, farmers no longer received the rich, nutritious silt the river had always carried with it. The silt they relied on to grow their crops is at the bottom of the reservoir. Instead, they began using chemical fertilizers, which have poisoned the river.

KEY WORDS

environmentalists people who worry that human activities may harm the environment

Anti-dam groups trying to stop the building of the Maheshwar Hydro-electric Dam, in India ▶

SAVE NARMADA
SAVE THE PEOPLE

Dams as flood defenses

Dams are all about controlling water. Some dams are built on low-lying land along the coast or next to rivers. These dams are designed to keep water out rather than keeping it in.

Levees and dikes

Levees are small embankment dams built alongside rivers to stop water from spilling over the banks when floodwaters raise the river level. Levees along the Mississippi River, in the U.S., are so wide that roads have been built on top of them. The whole system of levees on this river is more than 1,500 miles (2,400 km) long, which is longer than the Great Wall of China.

Dikes are similar to levees, but they protect low-lying land from flooding by the sea. In countries such as the Netherlands, dikes are also built to enclose an area of the sea. The seawater is then pumped out, leaving a piece of land called a polder, which can be used for farming or housing.

▲ Dikes in the Netherlands are thick walls of earth used to prevent flooding.

Flood barriers

In England, the Thames River flows through London and out into the North Sea. In the past, severe storms have driven the sea up the river, causing the river to spill over its banks and flood the heart of London. To solve this problem, the Thames flood barrier was built across the river. The barrier has 10 steel gates which can be raised and closed against the floodwaters.

The Thames flood barrier ▶

23

Hydro-electricity

Hydro-electric dams have a power station as part of their structure. The water is released from the reservoir and rushes down massive chutes into a turbine hall. When the water strikes the blades of the turbines, they spin. A generator turns this spinning movement into electricity, which is sent out through overhead powerlines to people's homes. The power station is usually a building at one end of the dam, or it might be inside a cave which has been blasted out of solid rock.

▼ **The generator hall at Bonneville Dam, Washington**

Beneath Elidir Mountain, in Wales, there are 10 miles (16 km) of underground water tunnels belonging to the Dinorwig hydro-electric power station. It took 1.1 million tons (1 million t) of concrete, 220,500 tons (200,000 t) of cement, and 4,960 tons (4,500 t) of steel to build the generator hall. Dinorwig's six generators stand inside one of the largest human-made caves in the world. It is known as Electric Mountain.

Cofferdams

A cofferdam is a temporary circular dam built in shallow water. The water is pumped out and the soft river mud is dug away until harder ground is felt. The bottom of the cofferdam is lined with concrete to waterproof it. Cofferdams are used mainly in bridge building. If the supports of a bridge are going to be standing in water, a cofferdam is built to keep the work area dry. A cofferdam built during the construction of the Golden Gate Bridge, in the U.S., was large enough to enclose a playing field.

Looking after dams

Once a dam has been built, it may take many months, or even years, for the reservoir to fill. When the reservoir is full, the **sluicegates** and spillways control the level and flow of the water through pipes and chutes. The sluices have screens across them to stop any plants or garbage from blocking the pipes and spillways.

When the water level is too high, spillways open to prevent water from lapping over the top of the dam. Spillways are designed to keep the water away from the base of the dam wall. When the water runs down a spillway, it does so at extremely high speed. If the water hits the dam wall continuously, it will wear the wall away. A spillway can be a pipe running from the reservoir through the dam itself and into the river. Water scientists, called hydrologists, control when the sluicegates are opened.

Releasing water through the sluicegates keeps the river clear by flushing any build-up of silt downstream.

These spillways are positioned up high so that water spurts out at very high speed.

Cracking

If a dam collapses, it releases all of its water at once. To avoid a catastrophic flood, the dam structure is checked regularly for cracks and movement. Engineers trained in rope-climbing can inspect the difficult-to-reach parts of a dam.

Checking is most important when a dam is new. The ground beneath the dam and the reservoir could shift because of the extra weight suddenly added on top of it. Inside the dam, there is a control room where instruments measure even the tiniest movement. Information is collected to see if the structure of the dam is working as the designers thought it would.

KEY WORDS

sluicegates gates that control the flow of water in a channel or spillway

DAMS THAT WENT WRONG

Early dams were sometimes washed away when floodwaters surged over the top of their earth embankments. Other dams have cracked during earthquakes. Modern dams are much stronger and more stable, and their water levels are carefully controlled. But not all modern dams have been successful.

Broken spillway gates

On July 17, 1995, a spillway gate in the Folsom Dam, in the U.S., broke open as it was being raised. This caused an uncontrolled waterfall as high as a five-story building to plunge down the face of the dam. Nearly half of the reservoir drained out through the broken gate before it could be repaired. Luckily, no major flooding was caused. The spillway gates roll up and down on giant metal pins like roller doors on a garage. The metal pins were becoming hot from the constant rubbing of the metal and this weakened the pins. The spillway gates are being redesigned, but it has cost millions of dollars to repair the dam.

◀ In 2002, the collapse of the Zeyzoun Dam in northern Syria caused a flood wave that killed more than 20 people and made thousands homeless.

Killer wave

In 1963, floodwater filled the reservoir of the 846-foot-high (258-m) Vaiont Dam, in Italy, to within 39 feet (12 m) of the top of the dam. When a huge chunk of mountainside above the reservoir slid into the water, it sent a wave as high as a 30-story building across the reservoir and over the top of the dam. The water raced downhill into villages, drowning 2,500 people. The arch dam itself survived.

China

In 1975, the Banqiao Dam and the Shimantan Dam, both in the same area of China, collapsed. It is thought that 230,000 people died because of flooding and, later, as a result of starvation and disease after the dams collapsed.

Three Gorges Dam

The Three Gorges Dam, which is expected to be finished by 2009, will be the most powerful hydro-electric dam in the world. It will be 600 feet (185 m) high and more than 1.4 miles (2 km) long, and create a reservoir 370 miles (600 km) long. The dam is designed to protect the area from the devastating floods that have killed 300,000 people in the last 100 years alone. However, earthquakes are common in the area, and many people believe that if an earthquake occurred, more than a million people would die. They believe that a series of smaller dams would be safer.

Environmentalists are worried that the dam will make some kinds of animals die out forever and trap pollution from China's largest industrial city, Congquing. More than one million people must leave their homes because the reservoir will flood their villages. Many ancient temples, burial grounds, and important **artifacts** will be lost beneath the water forever.

The Three Gorges Dam will be so big that if you were on the moon, you would be able to see it.

AMAZING DAMS

Many of the world's most amazing structures are dams. After the Great Wall of China, dams are the biggest human-made structures on Earth. Some dams are record-breakers because of their size or the immense amount of water they hold back. Others are famous for the amount of hydro-electric power they produce.

Most powerful hydro-electric dam

Until the Three Gorges Dam is finished in 2009, the Itaipu Dam, on the Parana River, on the Brazil–Paraguay border, is the most powerful hydro-electric dam in the world. The Itaipu Dam is a 4.8-mile-long (7.7-km) combination of hollow-concrete gravity and rockfill dams. Its 18 generators produce enough electricity to supply 25 percent of Brazil's power needs and 78 percent of Paraguay's.

Building the dam was not easy. Engineers had to divert the seventh largest river in the world. It took almost three years to carve a 1.3-mile-long (2-km), 300-foot-deep (91-m), 490-foot-wide (149-m) channel to take the river around the construction site. As the engineers chose a hollow gravity dam instead of a solid one, extra metal reinforcing was needed. The amount of iron and steel used in the dam would be enough to build 380 Eiffel Towers!

◀ The Guri Dam, in Venezuela, is the third most powerful hydro-electric dam in the world.

Dam facts and firsts

Here are some interesting facts and figures. There are many more you can find out about.

The world's biggest dam

The Syncrude Tailings Dam, in Canada, is the biggest dam in the world because it used the most materials to build it. Syncrude is not like any other dam. It is an embankment dam made by piling up the waste material dug from a nearby mine. The pile is pressed down by machines to waterproof and strengthen the dam. The reservoir contains water and sludge pumped from the mine to keep it dry enough for the miners to work in. There is enough material to make a heap 1.8 miles (3 km) high!

The world's tallest dams

Some dams have achieved record-breaking heights. When the Rogun Dam, in Tajikistan, is finished, it will be 1,099 feet (335 m) high, which is 151 feet (46 m) shorter than the Empire State Building. It is not yet completed, due to political troubles, earthquakes, and flooding, and has already needed some repairing.

Here is how the world's tallest dams look against some other famous structures in the world. ▼

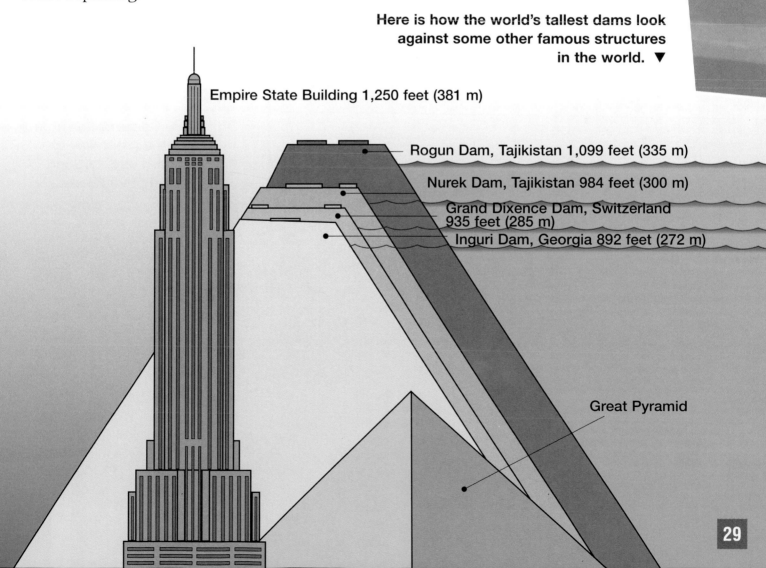

Empire State Building 1,250 feet (381 m)

Rogun Dam, Tajikistan 1,099 feet (335 m)

Nurek Dam, Tajikistan 984 feet (300 m)

Grand Dixence Dam, Switzerland 935 feet (285 m)

Inguri Dam, Georgia 892 feet (272 m)

Great Pyramid

USING MODELS TO LEARN ABOUT STRUCTURES

You can find out about some of the challenges engineers meet when they design and build a dam by using a construction set to build your own. Construction sets have beams and blocks that can be made into strong and stable shapes to build structures.

Strength and stability are just as important in a construction set as they are in a life-sized structure. Many of today's engineers and architects started with construction sets. They are still building with them—the construction sets just grew bigger.

◀ Construction sets are a great way to learn about strong and stable dams.

GLOSSARY

artifacts	objects, ornaments, or tools made by ancient people
beaver	a four-legged, furry animal which lives partly on land and partly in water, and which is found in Europe, Asia, and North America
bedrock	solid rock beneath the soil
brace	something fastened to an object to keep it stiff and straight, just like the braces worn on teeth
buttress	a support for a wall
cement	an ingredient in concrete which makes the concrete harden like stone
channel	a passage along which water flows
concrete	a building material made by mixing cement and sand or gravel with water
corrosive	a substance that eats away at metal and concrete
embankment	a ridge of earth or rocks made by humans to stop water from overflowing
engineers	people who design and build large structures
environmentalists	people who worry that human activities may harm the environment
face	the front of the dam
flexible	able to bend without breaking
foundations	a firm base upon which a structure is built
generators	machines that make electricity
geologists	scientists who study rocks and soil
gravity	a force that makes things fall when you drop them
groundworks	the preparation of the ground for a dam's foundations
irrigating	bringing water through pipes or ditches to water land
materials	anything used to make a structure
quarry	a place where stone is removed by digging or blasting
reinforced	made stronger
reservoir	a lake for storing water until it is needed
silt	tiny particles of rock washed down a river
sluicegates	gates that control the flow of water in a channel or spillway
stable	something that will not wobble or fall
structure	something that is made up of many parts joined together
temporary	for a short time only
turbines	machines that spin like wheels when water flows over them

INDEX